GW00643499

How to Talk to Mums

BY ALEC GREVEN

ILLUSTRATIONS BY KEI ACEDERA

HarperCollins *Children's Books*

First published in the UK by HarperCollins Children's Books

How to Talk to Mums
Text copyright © 2008 by Alec Greven
Illustrations copyright © 2008 by Kei Acedera

ISBN 978-0-00-731954-1
Typography by Ray Shappell
1 3 5 7 9 10 8 6 4 2

CONTENTS

INTRODUCTION

There are lots of things mums do that annoy you.
Such as making you do the laundry.
Who wants to sort your brother's underwear?
Or clean the mess that's in the living room.

But guess what?
Mums also do all sorts of things to help you out.
Mums take care of you and feed you and give you advice.
Being a mum is a really, really hard job because we
don't always follow directions and things can get wild.

Kids do lots of things that annoy mums.
You know what I am talking about.
But even when you annoy your mum, she still loves you.
That's the best part.

CHAPTER ONE

What's Up with Mum?

{ *Sometimes you think your mum is mean and wants to ruin your life.* }

Sometimes your mum seems like the most wonderful
woman in the world.
But sometimes you think she is mean
and wants to ruin your life.
Really, it is both.

You probably think your mum is wonderful
when she is doing something nice for you, like:

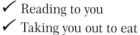

- ✓ Helping you with homework
- ✓ Letting you play all day
- ✓ Reading to you
- ✓ Taking you out to eat

You probably think your mum is trying to ruin your life when she makes you:

- ✓ Clean
- ✓ Rake leaves
- ✓ Go to bed early
- ✓ Eat broccoli

Or if she punishes you by:
✔ Sending you to your room
✔ Taking away your games and toys

The mum job is hard.
If you go to the dark side and cause trouble, she has to be tough.

So mums make your life easy and hard at the same time.
That's just the way it is.

CHAPTER TWO

What Mums Like

{ *When you clean up by yourself without being asked,*
you will probably get some big rewards. }

Mums like nice notes.
When you mess up,
write a note and say you are sorry.

Mums like hugs. Give lots of hugs
and not just to get what you want.

Mums like clean kids.
It will make your mum smile if you
take a shower and comb your hair.
They also like you to wash your hands a lot
and wear clean clothes.

Mums like polite kids. Try to have nice manners.
Use "please" and "thank you" and "may I."
Ask to be excused from the table and wipe your face.

A good way to surprise your mum and make her happy
is to clean up around the house,
like your room, the bathroom, or the living room.

When you clean up without being asked,
you will probably put Mum in a good mood, and that is great.
You might get some big rewards.

Some types of rewards are:
- ✓ Taking you to the movies
- ✓ Letting you stay up late
- ✓ Letting you have friends over

CHAPTER THREE

What Mums Don't Like

{ *Mums don't like to find weird stuff in your pockets.* }

Mums don't like it when you use your shirt as a napkin
or a handkerchief.

Mums don't like to find weird stuff in your pockets.
Make sure to empty them of things
that are alive or sticky or gross.

Mums don't like you to fight with your brother and sister.
They don't like you to whine or yell.

Mums don't like you to do bad pranks,
like tripping your brother or dumping water on him.

Mums don't like loose wildlife in the house.
But who doesn't like to catch things?
And of course if you catch stuff,
you want to keep it for a while.

But remember this important tip:
When you catch annoys, spiders, or snakes
and you want to bring them inside,
make sure you use a container with a lid.
Keep them locked down.

Some mums are easy-going. Some mums freak out a lot.
It helps you if you know what your mum likes and doesn't like.
If you understand your mum, you won't get in trouble as much.

CHAPTER FOUR

How Mums Annoy Their Kids

{ *Sometimes it seems like mums are obsessed with cleaning and chores.* }

Most kids don't care about things being clean, but mums do.
Sometimes it seems like mums are obsessed with
cleaning and chores.
Clean your room, clean the bathroom, clean your face.
Walk the dog. Put the dishes away.
Or the worst – clean the toilet.
All these things bore kids.

You need to be smart when your mum asks you to clean.
If it is a little mess, clean up without hesitation
and she will love it.
This is worth a lot because mums remember the good stuff you do.
Plus, you will probably get a lot of compliments and hugs.

Try to stay low and make little messes
so that your mum doesn't get mad.
If you do make a big mess,
clean it up immediately or your mum will go nuts.
And you will get in serious trouble!

If your mum asks you to clean your little brother's room, add some touches, like putting a rock under his pillow, just to give him a little punishment for having to clean his room.

But sometimes cleaning works out for you.
Every three out of four missing toys are found when cleaning huge messes!

CHAPTER FIVE

Excuses, Bribes, and the Backfire

{ Mums are smart cookies and they don't like excuses,
so I don't recommend them. }

Kids try and say no to Mum all the time.
You might try to protest or make up an excuse.
But beware of the backfire!
The backfire is when your plan goes very wrong.

When you try to get out of something your mum wants you to do,
95 per cent of the time you will get the backfire.

When you don't want to clean,
one way to say no is to try protesting.
Don't give up without a fight.
Here are ways to protest:
✓ But, but, but. But I need help.
✓ Why can't I do it later?
✓ But I am hungry.

TIP: *The backfire happens about 45 per cent of the time with Dad,
and maybe 1 per cent of the time with Grandma.
(Everybody knows that grandmas spoil you.)*

If you protest, you need to use caution.
You will probably make your mum mad, get in big trouble,
and still have to do that thing you don't want to do.
Backfire!

You could also try to make up an excuse,
like saying your stomach hurts to get out of doing chores.
But your mum will probably make you stay in bed
all day long doing nothing.
Backfire!

Try an excuse if you want,
but don't come crying to me when it doesn't work.
Mums are smart cookies and they don't like excuses,
so I don't recommend them.

Sometimes your mum asks you to do something
and offers you a bribe.
An example of a bribe is when your mum says,
"If you clean up the living room, we can go to the pool."

Maybe you think it isn't worth it
and you don't want to go to the pool *that* bad.
But if your mum asks you to do something and offers a bribe,
you might as well take it.
If you don't, she probably will get mad and make you do it anyway,
and then you don't get the treat.
Backfire!

CHAPTER SIX

How Kids Annoy Their Mums

{ *When you make concoctions with stuff like Mum's perfume or food, you are probably going to get in trouble.* }

Kids do a lot of things that annoy their mums.
You know the obvious things,
like fighting with your brother and sister and yelling.

But these aren't the only things.
Making stews, potions, and other concoctions is fun
because you mix all sorts of ingredients.
Usually it is best to use natural things
like leaves, grass, rocks, and stuff like that.

When you make concoctions with stuff
like Mum's perfume or food,
you are probably going to make her mad.
No more Miss Nice Mum for sure!

You will also get in trouble if you make a big mess,
use Mum's flowers, or make your concoctions
in Mum's things (like the birdbath or the fountain).

It is a good idea to ask your mum first
and try not to do undercover activities.
Undercover activities are when you don't ask your mum
and you try to hide it.
Mums do not like undercover concoctions.
But the funny part is she probably did it when she was a kid.

CHAPTER SEVEN

Why I Love My Mum

{ *Mums love you no matter what.* }

Mums really don't want to ruin your life.
Mums just want to help you succeed and be better.
They make you do things you don't want to do,
but they do all sorts of things to help you.

Mums read to you and play games with you.

Mums play football with you and camp out with you.
Mums fix broken things for you.
Mums drive you everywhere you need to go.
Mums take you on holiday.

Mums take care of you and feed you,
give you advice, help you with your homework,
and help you sort out problems.
Plus they love you no matter what.

Remember what your mum does for you
and what you can do to make her happy.

Even when you annoy each other,
you always love each other.
And that's the best part!

ACKNOWLEDGMENTS

For my mum,
of course!